The Pocket Budget Book

For those who live paycheck to paycheck

Asmeret Payne

Book 1 of the pocket budget books

ISBN:1548228885
ISBN-13:978-1548228880

DEDICATION

To my loving husband Jared
For always believing in me and putting up with me.

The Pocket Budget Book

CONTENTS

1 What is a Budget

A budget is a plan for your money what is spent where and how much. So we need some numbers to start with for the next month I want you to write down everything you spend your money on, **How much** you spent, **Where** you spent it from, **Which Tab** did it come from (checking, savings, credit card?), **When** you spent it, and what is the **New Total** in that account. If you were paid just write that in the how much you spent column but put a plus sign in front of the number so you remember. There will be some other columns but those are for later so just ignore them for now. Like this

Just Ignore this one for now |
V

How Much	Where	Which Tab	When	New Total	Group
35.62	Cafe	Checking	5/17	478.81	

Now it is your turn. Remember we are just making a starting point now so spend like you normally would.

How Much	Where	Which Tab	When	New Total	Group

How Much	Where	Which Tab	When	New Total	Group

How Much	Where	Which Tab	When	New Total	Group

How Much	Where	Which Tab	When	New Total	Group

How Much	Where	Which Tab	When	New Total	Group

How Much	Where	Which Tab	When	New Total	Group

2 Ok now what

Now that we have some numbers to work with the next thing we have to do is fill in that last column.

Remember this one that I told you to leave alone |

V

How Much	Where	Which Tab	When	New Total	Group

This is where we start to actually make a budget go back to all of the purchases you make over the last month. In the **Group** Column put: **FB** (Fixed bill or one that doesn't change month to month like Rent, Garbage, or minimum monthly payments), **VB** (Variable Bill or one that does change month to month like electric bill, gas), **Need** (Groceries, clothing), **IN** (income and this is whatever not just paychecks) and finally **EN** (this is entertainment like going to the movies, out to coffee or anything else you do for fun.) Go ahead and fill that out for everything you have done for the past month, I will wait.

Now we are going to total these up. Like this

FB	VB	Need	En	In
675	283	347	89	1412

Now it is your turn.

FB	VB	Need	En	In

And more math sorry. I will try to keep this simple since if you are like me the numbers will be depressing enough already, but don't worry that is what we are going to fix with this book. So take your **FB, VB,** and **Need** and add them together. So my example numbers would be 675+283+347= 1305.

Now your turn.

Your **FB**_____ + **VB** _____ +

Need _____=_____.

Now take your total Income **IN** and subtract that last number. so mine was 1412 - 1305 = 107.

Your **In** _____ - _____=

_____

Yeah I know that sitncks and that isn't including anything for fun. but stick with me we will fix that. so take that last number and take out $5. That is right just $5 for now. so my example numbers 107 - 5 = 102. This is your new entertainment budget. See totally doable right. It seems small but small victories are the way to go and we will build on that so we are only on page 17 and you have already saved. ;)

Now we need this entertainment budget to last all month so divide it by 4 and that is your fun budget for the week. So my sample is 102 / 4 = 25.50 each week.

Yours _____ / 4 = _____

I know that doesn't seem like much but next month will be better and I will show you a bunch of things that you can do for cheap or free as well.

One way to build on what you have is to stop useless things like late fees. I use Prism to track bills and paychecks, even ones that are already set for auto pay. It makes it easy to keep everything in one place, and they will remind you when bills are due and you can even pay right from the home screen. Displaying when your paychecks are coming in also helps not to overdraw, and get more fees that way.

Do whatever works for you just make sure to pay them on time and keep track of your balance.

Remember that $5? Well now I need you to put it somewhere safe. This is the start of your emergency fund. A free checking account that you do not keep the card to in your wallet would be good. Or I use Stash Http://get.stashinvest.com/asmeret430tw. This is my referral code and will earn us both $5. So I am being paid to tell you about it technically.

Stash is an investment account app. It also teaches you about stocks and bonds and the different types of investments as you use it. And for our purposes now there is no minimum balance, the first three months are free (it is only a dollar a month after that) and most important it takes a few days to get your money back. I know that sounds like a draw back but right now we want the money to be a little inaccessible.

Next we are going through your home to save on those utility bills. You can do a lot of this even if you Rent, but if this doesn't apply to you then just skip it and move on to the next chapter.

3 Utilities

http://www.apartmenttherapy.com/how-to-read-your-utility-bill-131512 does a pretty good job on breaking down how to read your utility bills. so if you need help I would recommend visiting his site.

I however am going to cover some tips and trick I have used to lower my Utility bills.

- ☐ Turn down your water heater if you have your own water heater chances are it is turned up way too high. The heater is how hot the water gets not how much there is. Turn it down so that the water only gets to the hottest you use dishes or showers for example. There is no reason to have it so high that the water coming out of the tap can burn you. Just turn it down you will have less household accidents either from burns or in my case crashing into things after jumping back from being burned.
- ☐ Put aerators on your faucets. These are tiny little rings you put on your water faucets to add air bubbles to the water. They actually increase the water pressure while using less water. Water bill goes down but pressure is up!
- ☐ Insulate your outlets. A few dollars and a screwdriver can make a big difference in your heating and air conditioning bill. Add these to all the outlets on exterior walls for more insulation or on interior walls to cut down on hearing everything the neighbors are doing.

- [ ] Curtains are more than just decorative thick curtains can save on heating and air conditioning as well. If you want the house cooler close the curtains during the day and open at night or the other way for warmth in winter.
- [ ] Turn off the lights. Or switch to lower wattage bulbs. LEDs are best on electric bills but make sure they don't give you a headache.
- [ ] Read your phone bill are you being charged for things you don't use? If so ditch it. If you are on a data plan see if there is a roll over option so at least it doesn't go away at the end of the month. After you have collected a bit of roll over try downgrading your data for a while.
- [ ] Ditch Cable, or Satellite TV and use a service like Netflix most of the channels have nothing on anyway. This one can easily save hundreds a month.
- [ ] If you have an attic add insulation
- [ ] Put a light sensitive nightlight under your thermostat at night the light will come on and heat up the thermostat effectively turning it down at night.
- [ ] Insulate the water heater
- [ ] Bare walls hang decorative quilts or blankets the extra insulation is nice too.
- [ ] If you have your own washer dryer put it on cold water it will save the dyes in your clothes and cut the heating bill.
- [ ] If you are cooking just for yourself or up to two others use a toaster oven instead of the regular oven it takes a lot less time to heat up and a lot less energy. Faster and cheaper no quality difference.
- [ ] Clean your dryer lint screen. Pull the lint off sure but then take it over to the sink every so often and

run it under the faucet if the water pools then there are microfibers blocking the airflow just scrub it gently with a dish brush and it should all come off. When the water runs straight through you are good. This will lower the electric bill and dry your clothes faster.

☐ Cover windows in winter they have kits you can buy but i prefer clear plastic drop cloth it is cheaper and thicker not as see through so it will block your view but not the light.

☐ If you go out to do laundry consider getting an apartment washer dryer they just plug into the faucet in the bathroom so it is good for renters.

☐ Use a humidifier in the winter the water moisture carries heat better and more effectively around your home and is better for you health wise.

☐ Change the furnace filter every few months. Cleaner air more efficient furnace.

☐ Clean the coils on the back of your refrigerator this will make your fridge more efficient.

☐ Clean out the inside of the fridge not just the shelves but wipe down the lining as well better airflow inside and a better seal will also make the fridge more efficient.

☐ Put a thermometer in the fridge you want the temperature to be between 32* and 40* Fahrenheit. For safe food storage.

☐ Same for the freezer it should be around 0* if you have a lot of icy build up that means it is set too low and needs to be defrosted and reset. This can save a lot on the power.

☐ Use mirrors to decorate. It makes small spaces seem bigger and increases the light in the room with no extra electricity.

❑ Don't Place Hot Foods in a Fridge. Allowing foods to cool to room temperature ensures your unit won't have to work as hard.

❑ Thaw in the Fridge. Frozen items throw off cold air into the fridge, helping to keep things cool.

❑ Make Your Own Ice. Automatic ice makers use unnecessary energy and are prone to breakdown. Likewise, cold air can be lost through in-door dispensers with poor seals.

❑ Skip the Dry Cycle. Open the dishwasher door and allow dishes to air-dry.

❑ Use the Oven Light. Instead of opening the door to check if foods are done, switch on the oven light to see inside without losing heat.

❑ Use the Correct-Sized Burner. Large burners under small pots or pans waste heat.

❑ Use an Electric Kettle. Electric kettles boil water faster and more efficiently than stovetop kettles. Use them for making tea or boiling water for small meals.

❑ Cook on the Top Rack of the Oven. Keep your food closer to the heating element and cut cooking time by up to 20 percent.

❑ Run appliances at night to take advantage of non peak hour rates. Rearrange your furniture to take advantage of airflow vents pour into the room instead of the back of your couch.

❑ Go with and LED TV instead of a Plasma they use far less electricity.

4 Tips and Tricks for Everything else

- ☐ Make your own coffee instead of getting it out
- ☐ Bring bag lunches to work.
- ☐ Use Pokemon Go or other game instead of the gym.
- ☐ Want a cheap date picnic in the park
- ☐ Invite friends over for game night.
- ☐ Make gifts don't buy them
- ☐ Send an ecard a lot of these are really funny
- ☐ Dont' shop for groceries hungry
- ☐ List shopping for groceries make a list then set it down the next day cross out anything you don't need. People use to do this one during the Great depression it works
- ☐ Clean out your closet and have a yard sale
- ☐ Rent games you only want to play once buy what you will play over and over
- ☐ Swap books movies and cds online
- ☐ Change the air filter on your car
- ☐ Cancel all unused club memberships
- ☐ Shop used but make sure you are saving money a few thrift stores price the same as new so check.
- ☐ Remove card numbers from online accounts don't save the info it will make you stop and think if your really want it.
- ☐ Have your holidays a day late. Valentines candy is on sale and the restaurants are not as crowded besides you just might get holiday pay for working.
- ☐ Go generic brands spend most of their money making you think that they are better but sometimes they just aren't.

- ☐ Check out free events in your town
- ☐ Library use it. Some even have console video games you can just check out movies music all kinds of things.
- ☐ Go the speed limit it uses less gas you get pulled over less often and most traffic lights are programed so that you will hit more greens if you are going the speed limit so you will actually get where you are going faster.
- ☐ Read a book!!!!!!!!
- ☐ Have a vegetarian night meat is expensive
- ☐ Use a surge protector This is a must it will save your very expencive stuff.
- ☐ Have a pet cats are very self sufficient eat little and provide hours of entertainment and incentive to stay home rather than going out.
    - ☐ I use the wood pellet litter it is light cheap and very good at odor control. Also environment friendly.

5 Now lets try this again

How Much	Where	Which Tab	When	New Total	Group

How Much	Where	Which Tab	When	New Total	Group

How Much	Where	Which Tab	When	New Total	Group

How Much	Where	Which Tab	When	New Total	Group

6 Did you do better?

So the math again Total up all the different categories.

FB	VB	Need	En	In

And do the adding **FB+VB+Need=**_____

FB_____+VB_____+

Need _____ = _____

Then take your income and subtract.

IN_____ - _____ =

_____

Does this look better than last time? Good so this time we are going to do something a little different. How did your fun budget work? if it was ok then only add a few dollars to it, if you couldn't stick to it but tried then add a little more. Just make sure that you are putting at least $10, that is right $10 not $5 in your Stash. I am going to call it stash but whatever worked for you piggy bank whatever.)

Congratulations you just tripled your savings!

Now we are going to keep up the work pack away everything that is not a part of your fun budget and don't skimp on the fun budget. You won't stick to it if it is not fun. If your fun budget is not enough then adjust it next time but keep at it. Once have reached $1000 we will move on to the next step.

7 Let's work on passive income.

Passive income is a great way to save money. One site I have used in the past is InboxDollars. My referal code is https://www.inboxdollars.com/?r=ref30288274&s=7 again we both get $5 if you use it. So there is that. I have used them before and they are ok as far as these things go. They do pay out I have received several checks. I wouldn't do everything though you can end up signing up for a lot of spam if you are not careful I would stick to the surveys videos and emails.

There are a lot of passive income apps out there. I would love to hear which ones you use and how they worked out. Just remember to add the passive income to your Stash, minus a little something for the win.

You can also do odd jobs and side projects my mother used to make earrings to sell at craft fairs. I have even heard of people opening beetle farms to sell to pet stores.

While in college I sold used books online. I would go out to yard sales and pick up boxes of books and list them individually online. It was never much but it helped.

There are all kinds of things you can do ebay and etsy are good choices as well. Check out if grocery stores in your area are doing monopoly games or anything like that just do your regular shopping and collect the game pieces. don't use them instead post them on ebay. You will be amazed at what random hould hold items people will buy.

Just find what works for you and don't forget to celebrate the little things.

Try brian storming your oen ideas. What is your area of expertise? What do you like to do? Chances are there is a way to make at least a little money at it.

_____

_____

_____

_____

_____

_____

_____

_____

_____

_____

_____

_____

_____

_____

_____

_____

_____

_____

_____

_____

_____

_____

_____

8 More budget sheets and Tips / Tricks

Take a hard look at your cell phone provider are you really using all your data every month? Is there a cheaper option? Talk to a representative they might just cut you a deal rather than risk losing you as a customer.

How Much	Where	Which Tab	When	New Total	Group

See if you can find a way to earn money for the things you already do like rebates on groceries.

How Much	Where	Which Tab	When	New Total	Group

Try rags instead of paper towels. If you have an old Tee shirt with a hole in it you have a whole pile of rags to use around the house. Or socks with holes (Although I would definitely wash them first.) Just keep a bag or something to collect the dirty ones in and throw them in with your laundry.

How Much	Where	Which Tab	When	New Total	Group

When Grocery shopping check the price per unit as well as the item price it should be on the label. Make sure you are really getting the best price.

How Much	Where	Which Tab	When	New Total	Group

FB	VB	Need	En	IN

How are you doing? Have you checked on your Stash?

FB _____ **+ VB** _____ **+**

Need _____ **=** _____

IN _____ **-** _____**=**

_____ **- EN** _____**=**

_____ add to Stash.

How are you doing? Better than you thought?
Keep it up you are doing great.

9 More Sheets and Cheats

Keep healthy snacks in the car or your bag to cut down on impulse take out.

How Much	Where	Which Tab	When	New Total	Group

Don't buy things just because they are on sale or because you have a coupon. Stores set these up to encourage people to buy. Make sure it was already on your list.

How Much	Where	Which Tab	When	New Total	Group

Don't throw food out if those veggies look a little old then try dehydrating them. Cut them up and dehydrate then you can throw them in with whatever you are making for dinner. Dehydrators are not that expensive and can save you a lot in the long run.

How Much	Where	Which Tab	When	New Total	Group

It is pretty easy to score free stuff just look on Craigslist or Facebook often has local free or cheap pages. Try looking around to see if you can get it free first.

How Much	Where	Which Tab	When	New Total	Group

FB	VB	Need	En	IN

How are you doing? Have you checked on your Stash?

FB _____ **+ VB** _____ **+**

Need _____ **=** _____

IN _____ **-** _____ **=**

_____ **- EN** _____ **=**

_____ add to Stash.

How are you doing? Better than you thought?
Keep it up you are doing great.

10 Even More Sheets and Cheats

Save your spare change it adds up. Try a clear jar so you can see it rack up the dough.

How Much	Where	Which Tab	When	New Total	Group

Most people use way too much soap and shampoo try using very little. I know it seems silly but my husband and I tried more than a dozen different brands of detergent until we finally realised that the white stuff on our clothes was soap that wasn't coming off because we were using what it said on the package. The brands want you to use it up so you buy more, but it hardly takes any to really get your stuff clean.

How Much	Where	Which Tab	When	New Total	Group

If you go over budget it is ok we all make mistakes just try to get back on track.

How Much	Where	Which Tab	When	New Total	Group

You are entitled to a free credit report once a year. Make sure that it is accurate you might be paying more than you have to because of false reporting.

How Much	Where	Which Tab	When	New Total	Group

FB	VB	Need	En	IN

How are you doing? Have you checked on your Stash?

FB _____ + **VB** _____ +

Need _____ = _____

IN _____ - _____ =

_____ - **EN** _____ =

_____ add to Stash.

How are you doing? Better than you thought?
Keep it up you are doing great.

11 Keep it up!

If there is a recycling plant around try collecting cans both your own and your neighbors. I know it is a little intimidating to ask for them but a lot of people will set them aside for you. Then just make it a part of your weekly routine.

How Much	Where	Which Tab	When	New Total	Group

Do your own taxes. I know it looks very intimidating but there are step by step guides at the local library. And don't forget to check all the credits you might get more than you think.

How Much	Where	Which Tab	When	New Total	Group

Here is a simple one Drink Water from the tap. It is already paid for.

How Much	Where	Which Tab	When	New Total	Group

Start a window garden. Most vegetables are not worth it unless you have a big lawn but simple herbs are a great addition to the table and easy to grow. Also some vegetables like celery and leeks can be grown on the counter. when you are cutting them up for dinner just save the bottom and put it in a jar of shallow water. That's it easy right.

How Much	Where	Which Tab	When	New Total	Group

FB	VB	Need	En	IN

How are you doing? Have you checked on your Stash?

FB _____ **+ VB** _____ **+**

Need _____ **=** _____

IN _____ **-** _____ **=**

_____ **- EN** _____ **=**

_____ add to Stash.

How are you doing? Better than you thought?
Keep it up you are doing great.

12 On a roll.

Stop using dryer sheets entirely just ball up several rags in a clean sock . Throw two of these in the dryer and presto. Better for your dryer too.

How Much	Where	Which Tab	When	New Total	Group

When shopping for just a few items don't get a cart or evan a basket just pick them up. You won't be tempted to get more because you can't carry it.

How Much	Where	Which Tab	When	New Total	Group

Shop for budget gift cards online then go shopping.

How Much	Where	Which Tab	When	New Total	Group

Try cash instead of a card you will see the money go out and not want to spend it. Likewise if you can carry larger bills so you won't want to break them.

How Much	Where	Which Tab	When	New Total	Group

FB	VB	Need	En	IN

How are you doing? Have you checked on your Stash?

FB _____ **+ VB** _____ **+**

Need _____ **=** _____

IN _____ **-** _____**=**

_____ **- EN** _____**=**

_____ add to Stash.

How are you doing? Better than you thought?
Keep it up you are doing great.

13. 7 down 5 to go

Have you tried carpooling?

How Much	Where	Which Tab	When	New Total	Group

Call your insurance company it never hurts
to see if you can get a better deal.

How Much	Where	Which Tab	When	New Total	Group

Don't buy alcohol or cigarettes they are expensive over time.

How Much	Where	Which Tab	When	New Total	Group

Sign up for a gas reward card that works with your grocery store.

How Much	Where	Which Tab	When	New Total	Group

FB	VB	Need	En	IN

How are you doing? Have you checked on your Stash?

FB _____ **+ VB** _____ **+**

Need _____ **=** _____

IN _____ **-** _____**=**

_____ **- EN** _____**=**

_____ add to Stash.

How are you doing? Better than you thought?
Keep it up you are doing great.

14 Even More Sheets and Cheats

Try a no spend day. Or even better yet only one spending day a week

The Pocket Budget Book

How Much	Where	Which Tab	When	New Total	Group

When going out to eat order water. Or even an appetizer instead of an entre.

How Much	Where	Which Tab	When	New Total	Group

Try ebooks you can download the programs to read them free and a lot of the classics are free as well.

How Much	Where	Which Tab	When	New Total	Group

I know this one sounds counter intuitive but go for quality rather than quantity. One good pair of shoes will last you longer than two cheap pair.

How Much	Where	Which Tab	When	New Total	Group

FB	VB	Need	En	IN

How are you doing? Have you checked on your Stash?

FB _____ **+ VB** _____ **+**

Need _____ **=** _____

IN _____ **-** _____**=**

_____ **- EN** _____**=**

_____ add to Stash.

How are you doing? Better than you thought?
Keep it up you are doing great.

15 Doing Good

Just say no to that candy bar at the checkout lane. or better yet get one bag of candy and put it in the freezer. take out a piece when you want it. The out of sight out of mind bit kicks in and the cold is more refreshing.

How Much	Where	Which Tab	When	New Total	Group

The same goes for soda only I would put
them in the fridge.

How Much	Where	Which Tab	When	New Total	Group

Try making your own pizzas instead of ordering. Also using tomato paste to make sauce instead of buying ready made.

How Much	Where	Which Tab	When	New Total	Group

Try more simple outfits that you can mix
and match.

How Much	Where	Which Tab	When	New Total	Group

FB	VB	Need	En	IN

How are you doing? Have you checked on your Stash?

FB _____ **+ VB** _____ **+**

Need _____ **=** _____

IN _____ **-** _____**=**

_____ **- EN** _____**=**

_____ add to Stash.

How are you doing? Better than you thought?
Keep it up you are doing great.

16. 10 down 2 to go

If you need a doctor schedule an appointment instead of going to the ER. It will save you a lot of money and often same day appointments are available.

How Much	Where	Which Tab	When	New Total	Group

Exercise regularly it is a lot cheaper to stay healthy.

How Much	Where	Which Tab	When	New Total	Group

Zip up your pants before washing so that the zipper doesn't cut up your other clothes.

How Much	Where	Which Tab	When	New Total	Group

When buying online shop for the specific item you want rather than by category. Statistics say you will spend less money.

How Much	Where	Which Tab	When	New Total	Group

FB	VB	Need	En	IN

How are you doing? Have you checked on your Stash?

FB _____ **+ VB** _____ **+**

Need _____ = _____

IN _____ - _____=

_____ - **EN** _____=

_____ add to Stash.

How are you doing? Better than you thought?
Keep it up you are doing great.

17 Almost there

Sell your photos online sites like IStock want your photos as long as they met certain guidelines.

How Much	Where	Which Tab	When	New Total	Group

Start a website or blog.

How Much	Where	Which Tab	When	New Total	Group

Have you ever heard of secret shopping? Big stores will hire you to shop there and report your experience.

How Much	Where	Which Tab	When	New Total	Group

Sell your services on fiverr or craigslist.

How Much	Where	Which Tab	When	New Total	Group

FB	VB	Need	En	IN

How are you doing? Have you checked on your Stash?

FB _____ **+ VB** _____ **+**

Need _____ **=** _____

IN _____ **-** _____**=**

_____ **- EN** _____**=**

_____ add to Stash.

How are you doing? Better than you thought?
Keep it up you are doing great.

18. Last one!

You can try being a driver for Lyft or Uber

How Much	Where	Which Tab	When	New Total	Group

If you are not going to be home for a while then you can rent it out on airbnb.

How Much	Where	Which Tab	When	New Total	Group

If you live in a busy area you can actually rent out your driveway on just park.

How Much	Where	Which Tab	When	New Total	Group

Do favors for people at work and ask for small ones in return it can actually lead to a promotion.

How Much	Where	Which Tab	When	New Total	Group

FB	VB	Need	En	IN

How are you doing? Have you checked on your Stash?

FB _____ **+ VB** _____ **+**

Need _____ **=** _____

IN _____ **-** _____**=**

_____ **- EN** _____**=**

_____ add to Stash.

How are you doing? Better than you thought?
Keep it up you are doing great.

19 Well you made it to the end of your first year on a budget.

How did you do? How is your Stash? If it still needs some work then just keep at it you know what to do now. If you have hit that seemingly magic $1000. Then you are ready to move on to that amazing next stage of paying off all your debt. Sound impossible? Well I bet living on a budget for a full year sounded pretty impossible before reading and working in this book, but here you are!

ABOUT THE AUTHOR

Asmeret Payne is a Filmmaker, Artist, and Writer. She received her bachelor's degree of Film and Art from University of Alaska Fairbanks on May 10th of 2015. She is the former president of University of Alaska's film club. She is a member in good standing of the National Society of Collegiate Scholars as well as Golden Key International Honors Society. Her short film *Cassandra's Dollhouse* won best in show at the Western Nevada Community College Art show and will be featured in the Thaw Out FIlm Festival 2015 as well as *The Muse* and *Dinner For Two*. Both short films premiered at the Thaw Out Film Festival as well. Asmeret Payne currently resides in North Pole Alaska.